THE STORY OF DHIRUBHAI AMBANI

AN INDIAN INDUSTRIALIST

SUSHMITA DUTTA

Published by True Sign Publishing House
Address: SY. No. 21/2 & 21/3, Sonnenahalli,
Krishnarajapura, Bengaluru,
Karnataka - 560049 India
E-mail: truesignbooks@gmail.com
Website: www.truesign.in

**The Story Of Dhirubhai Ambani
An Indian Industrialist**

Author: Sushmita Dutta

ISBN:978-93-5805-343-2

First Edition: 2023

CONTENTS

Introduction

Dhirajlal Hirachand Ambani, fondly called Dhirubhai Ambani, was an Indian industrialist who built from scratch India's largest privately controlled corporate empire. With his intelligent and innovative mind and knowledge about the stock market and how it can impact an economy, he put India on the global map. He took the world by storm when he founded **Reliance Industries** which served as India's largest exporter. It was the first Indian company that was privately owned to be featured on **Fortune 500**. This multinational conglomerate, headquartered in Mumbai, has diverse businesses including energy, petrochemicals, natural gas, retail, telecommunications, mass media, and textiles.

After his death in 2016, he was honoured posthumously with the **Padma Vibhushan**, India's second-highest civilian honour for his contributions to trade and industry.

"Think big, think fast, think ahead. Ideas are no one's monopoly."
Dhirubhai Ambani (insert picture of Dhirubhai Ambani)

Chapter - 1

Early Life and Education

Born to Hirachand Govardhandas Ambani and Jamunaben Ambani on 28th December, 1932 in Chorwad, Junagadh (present–day Gujarat) Dhirubhai was the third of five children. His father was a schoolteacher and his mother a housewife. Hirachand Ambani belonged to the Baniya community and played a significant role in his children's education. He was raised along with his two brothers – Ramanikbhai and Natubhai, and two sisters – Trilochanaben and Jasuben. As Dhirubhai's father was an ordinary teacher and the breadwinner of the family, it was difficult for him to manage and bear the expenses of such a large family. At times, the family did not have the money to fulfill their basic needs so Dhirubhai's mother borrowed money from the neighborhood. Dhirubhai grew up in a family that had modest means, prompting him to get his first job at the tender age of 16.

Dhirubhai studied in a local village school until the fifth standard. Later, he was sent to the **"Bahadur Khanji High School"** in Junagadh to pursue further studies.

During his childhood days, Dhirubhai was a naughty, playful and a fun-loving child who participated and performed exceptionally well in co-curricular activities. He was not good at studies and did not get good grades, not because he didn't attend school lessons, but because he didn't enjoy mugging up things and rote learning.

Even in his younger years he was righteous and possessed leadership qualities. At the age of 16, he showed great interest in socialism and politics, and visionised a developed India. One such incident which describes his leadership qualities has been narrated below:

During his school days, Junagarh was a princely state under the rule of the Nawab. The Nawab was required to merge the state with the Indian

Union after the **Indian Independence Act** was passed. But the Nawab declined to do so. As a result, when India was celebrating its independence on August 15, 1947 the people of Junagarh were not allowed to celebrate and were even told to stay indoors.

Dhirubhai ignored the ordinance and along with his schoolmates decided to perform a flag ceremony. They sang patriotic songs and handed out candy. Here he gave his first short speech, which was described as passionate and full of fervour.

Dhirubhai was detained but did not give up and refused to plead innocent. Later that night he was released, When he went back home he received a hero's welcome from his schoolmates.

Praja Mandal

Resistance grew in the region and Dhirubhai decided to join the **Praja Mandal** movement. He made posters in secret hideouts and distributed illegal newspapers and flyers with his school bag. At one point the pressure from the people was so great that the Nawab fled. Soon after, Junagarh joined the Indian Union. Later, Dhirubhai said that it was one of the most exciting days of his life.

Political ambitions of Dhirubhai Ambani

Shortly after this event, a new student movement was established in the city. Dhirubhai again became the leader, which eventually caught the attention of the local political leaders. He was very attracted to politics because it was a way to contribute to the development of a new India.

When the Municipal elections were held in Junagarh, Dhirubhai decided to campaign for the socialists, who had recently split from the Congress. He was specially attracted to political figures like Jawaharlal Nehru and Sardar Patel.

His father and older brother strongly opposed his participation in the campaign, partly because he had failed the entrance exam in school. Dhirubhai reassured them by saying that he would pass the exam next time, despite his participation in the campaign.

The candidates for whom Dhirubhai had campaigned won and he was delirious. He was immediately invited to join the **Socialist Party**. However, he felt he had bigger things to do and kindly declined the invitation.

Even before the results of his entrance exam were known, his father called him and said that he could no longer work due to his deteriorating health and that Dhirubhai would no longer be able to study, but that he was needed to help earn money. Dhirubhai replied that he would do what was expected of him. Ramnikbhai had already secured a job in Aden. Dhirubhai had to give up his education and political interests and drop out of school in the tenth standard.

Chapter - 2

Early Career

His first business venture

With only a 10th standard degree in hand, he immediately started working on a fruit and snack truck. He could earn a little money from this, but it was insufficient. He was determined to change his situation and circumstances with his hard work.

Suddenly, he found an opportunity when religious tourism was evolving near his hometown. His target market was the pilgrims at Girnar in the state of Gujarat. He began selling bhajiyas and other food products there by using his wits. Being a popular tourist site, there were a lot of visitors almost every day, which allowed Dhirubhai to make a considerable amount of money.

But with such a seasonal industry, they seldom ever turned a profit. This enterprise was likewise short-lived, and Dhirubhai's father counselled him to quit and look for employment after several failures.

Early Career Abroad

At the age of 16, he ventured overseas for the first time to the British colony of Aden (now Yemen) in search of job and opportunity. He worked for **A. Besse and Co.** as a dispatch clerk beside his brother, Ramnikbhai for a salary of only Rs.300. In the 1950s, this organization was one of the largest transcontinental trading firms east of Suez. It was during his tenure at this company that he learned trading, accounting and the intricacies of business skills.

His business skills was evident even in those early years. During that period, there was a firm called **Silver bullion**.This company used to sell metal in bulk. Exhibiting his innovative qualities, he thought of selling silver by melting it and claiming that it was silver in its purest form and then selling them at a large sum of money.

Dhirubhai purchased rials in bulk, melted them, and sold them on the **London Stock Exchange**. He made small profits, but it was easy money. Within three months of operation, Yemen's treasury officials noticed the shortage of coins in their country, and Dhirubhai's business of melting and selling coins ended. However, by the end of this time, Dhirubhai had already generated a few lakhs profit.

For a brief period he worked with **Shell Oil Agents** as a gas-station attendant and earned his first salary of INR 300 from this company. A couple of years later, the company became a distributor for **'Shell'** products and Dhirubhai was promoted to manage the company's oil-filling station at the port of Aden. It was here that he dreamed of setting up and owning a refinery, which he later realised with his petrochemicals venture.

Dhirubhai Ambani Worked for Free!

Dhirubhai had a lot of interest in speculation trading but had nominal funds to practice it. So, he worked for a Gujarati trading firm for free because he wanted to learn about speculation.

After he learned more about speculative trading, he started speculating on the purchase and sales of all types of goods. However, as Dhirubhai didn't have many funds to invest, he borrowed money from shopkeepers and friends on simple terms that "he would split the profit among the investors while bearing the loss alone."

Dhirubhai's unusual way of learning business by having expensive tea at expensive restaurants

Dhirubhai read lots of books that included topics ranging from history to psychology. However, there's a unique way Dhirubhai learned more about business – by drinking tea at expensive restaurants!

When Dhirubhai was working in **"A. Besse & Co.,"** the price of one cup of tea for the workers was 25 paise. However, he went to an expensive restaurant where the same cup of tea was Rs.1 (100 paise). He did so because he knew only the rich people came there. Dhirubhai heard conversations of those people and gathered business knowledge through them.

Chapter - 3

Marriage, Family and Children

Returned to India for Marriage

In 1955, at the age of 23, Dhirubhai tied the knot with Kokilaben. She was from Jamnagar (Gujarat) and was 21 years old at that time. She was a simple household lady who knew sewing and embroidery and belonged to a middle-class family.

Kokilaben played a vital role in Dhirubhai's success and supported him throughout his entire journey. Dhirubhai shared everything regarding his projects, encouraged her to learn English, and filled her with knowledge.

After two years on 19th April 1957, Kokilaben gave birth to Mukesh Ambani in Aden.

Back to Yemen

After marriage with Kokilaben, Dhirubhai had to get back to work in Aden. Until now, Dhirubhai had done well at the "A. Besse & Co." so he was promoted to the oil filling station at a new harbor.

In the initial days, Dhirubhai couldn't take his wife along with him, so there was a long-distance relationship between both of them. But soon, both of them reunited in Aden.

In 1958, Dhirubhai and his family came back to India and settled in Bombay. After shifting to India, their family grew and his wife gave birth to Anil and their two sisters, Nina and Dipti Ambani.

Kokilaben's journey

As Dhirubhai nurtured his empire, Kokilaben started changing from her cocooned, conservative Gujarati upbringing. She even appointed a teacher at home to learn English. But her public appearances were restricted to attending annual general body meetings of Reliance. She was content to be a bystander along with her daughters and bahus as her husband and sons faced a volley of questions from shareholders.

"When I got married to Dhirubhai in 1955, I had not even dreamt that my life would change so much. I saw Bombay for the first time. While going to Aden, I marvelled at the steamer, which was to take me there. Life was so different as compared to Jamnagar or other places but Dhirubhai was my guide. Aden was a turning point in the real sense for me."

When I recall my earlier years, a number of anecdotes come back to me. "Like the time when I was in Chorwad (in Gujarat) living there after my marriage. Dhirubhai had written a letter to me from Aden, which said, "Kokila, I have bought a car and I will come to fetch you in that car. Can you guess what is the colour of the car?" He then added, "it is black, like me." I liked his sense of humour the most. He came to pick me up in that car when I reached Aden. So it was a bullock cart at Chorwad, car at Aden and plane and helicopter in Bombay."

Whether it was in a two-bedroom chawl near Babulnath Temple, a six-storeyed apartment at Usha Kiran or the 14-storeyed Sea Wind, Kokilaben has stood by the values she upholds.

In the later years, Kokilaben always spoke of her husband's support that got her through tough times away from her family in India and how she cherished the time spent in those early years.

Chapter - 4

Birth of Reliance Industries

Dhirubhai finally comes back to India

By the end of the 1950s, the Yemenese independence movement had become powerful, and it was clear that British rule would not last any longer. Therefore, Indian communities of Hindus and Gujaratis living in Yemen started moving to Britain and India.

Now Dhirubhai had an option to choose between London and India. His friends suggested migration to London because of better opportunities. But Dhirubhai decided to return to India because he knew that India would grow massively in the upcoming years.

Finally, in 1958, Dhirubhai Ambani returned to Bombay, India, with his wife, little money, and zero connections. He settled with his family in a two-room chawl.

Dhirubhai wanted to start a business right away. He even explored multiple options, but he knew he didn't have enough savings to do the business he really wanted to do. So, he decided to start a company in partnership.

His first office

In the 1960s, Dhirubhai started **"Reliance Commercial Corporation"** in partnership with his second cousin, Champaklal Damani who lived with him in Yemen. This firm was to import polyester yarn and export spices to Yemen. The initial investment was Rs.15,000.

Reliance Commercial Corporation initially started as an exporter of spices. Dhirubhai went to Bombay's spice market and collected quotations for purchasing spices in bulk.

His first office was set up at **Masjid Bunder** on Narsinatha street. It was a 350 sq ft room with a telephone, one table and three chairs. Initially, they had two assistants to help them with their business. It was at this tiny office that he began building a team that would continue to stay with the organization for years to come. The team included his nephew Rasikbhai Meswani, his younger brother Ramnikbhai Nathubahi, and two former schoolmates. The team together usually carried out their tasks around the streets of Pydhonie.

Those days, **foreign exporters complained** a lot about the quality of supplies from India being lower than promised quality. Dhirubhai saw this problem as an opportunity and offered exporters to give up payment if the commodities were of poor quality.

Dhirubhai's offer built his reputation among the exporters, and the business started growing at an exponential rate. Soon, he started dealing with exporters in every possible commodity they required from India.

Emerging Interest in Yarn Trading

Dhirubhai realized that the business of commodities trading was coming to an end. Some of his friends in the yarn industry told him there were considerable profits in yarn import-export.

The dominance of the yarn industry by reputed firms like **Forbes Gokak** and sudden price fluctuations in the yarn market made the industry super-risky. But, as you know, Dhirubhai was fearless! He still wanted to get into the yarn industry.

Journey in the Yarn Industry

Dhirubhai had now entered into the yarn industry. In the beginning, he analyzed the yarn industry. Started the trade by purchasing small quantities and gradually moved onto bulk purchasing. While Dhirubhai was in the yarn business, he experienced a shortage of money. So, he solved this problem by borrowing money from Gujarati contractors, brokers, and merchants at reasonable interest rates. Sometimes, he applied his Aden trick of bearing the loss himself while splitting the profit.

Several people tried to pull down Dhirubhai in business due to envy, but he always stood firm, and Reliance Commercial Corporation kept growing.

Moved to a Better House

Dhirubhai's business was doing well, and his family was expanding. Anil Ambani was born in 1959, followed by Dipti and Nina Ambani in 1961 and 1962. By this time, he had left his two-room apartment and moved to a better apartment with them.

Split of Dhirubhai Ambani and Champaklal Damani

In 1965, Champaklal Damani and Dhirubhai Ambani ended their partnership and Dhirubhai started on his own. It is believed that both had different temperaments and different takes on how to conduct business. While Dhirubhai was a risk-taker who believed in building yarn inventories, Champaklal was a cautious trader who opposed stocking yarn.

Chapter - 5

Business Developments

Initial Years

Dhirubhai was a shrewd businessman who was willing to take risks and was aware of the importance of marketing. He understood the need to build inventories in order to generate an income. Armed with this knowledge, he decided to launch **Reliance Commercial Corporation.** In the beginning, he was not focused on money, instead he was focused on the quality of the spices which he was trading. He was trading jaggery, betel, sugar, nuts along with spices to the Gulf Emirates.

Once he was confident that his company had expanded as far as commodities was concerned, he began to direct his attention to synthetic textiles. He set his eyes on **backward integration** and opened the first **Reliance textile mill** in 1966. The company eventually transformd into a petrochemical giant and went on to add power generation and plastics into its offerings.

Growth in Business

He entered the yarn trading business with a small start-up and then succeeded to make some bigger deals. In addition to this, he was elected as the Director of the association of **Bombay Yarn Merchants**. According to many experts, it was the yarn trading market that provided ample wealth to Dhirubhai Ambani. In this business, due to the insights that he gained from his past experiences, he cracked two deals that provided a huge amount of money to him. This enabled him to set-up his upcoming firm which was to be named as **Reliance Textiles** in the future. And finally, he got his plan implemented and started to build a textile mill in Ahmedabad, Gujarat in the Naroda region of Ahmedabad.

Business Establishment

He used to travel between Bombay and Ahmedabad every weekend to check the progress and the kinds of problems encountered by the workers. His target was to produce the finest quality of nylon in a short period of time along with huge quantities. He was also conscious of the safety of the workers in the factory. In order to construct the factory within the stipulated deadlines he increased the labour force. At the same time during the construction of the factory, the value of the rupee also came down which impacted his project in terms of the economy. But as he was firm in his decisions, he continued with his project despite the risk.

In August 1966, the construction work of the factory was complete. In addition to this, the types of equipment were also installed along with the major pieces of machinery. In 1966 on 1st January the factory started work with only 35 men who were hired from Calcutta, Bombay and Indore. Initially, there was a problem in the conduct of business but later on, after some months in 1967, the factory started to deliver what it was built for. Many buyers refrained to buy fabric from Reliance as there were many big mills that was well-established.

Business Expansion

Incorporation of Reliance Industries Ltd. and Vimal

But Dhirubhai was not the one to accept defeat. Therefore, he came into the market by himself and started selling his fabric directly to the retailers. After some time, his fabric was in demand all over the market and the demand increased with time. This fabric was **"Vimal"** and it became the fast-selling fabric at that time. Under the name of the label, 'Vimal' other clothing items like sarees, dresses, shawls and suits were sold. By 1972, Reliance was a huge company and was growing at a very fast pace. On May 8th 1973, Dhirubhai changed the name **Reliance Commercial Corporation** to **Reliance Industries.**

During 1981, his elder son Mukesh Ambani joined the business and focused on **backward integration**, and expanded textiles dealing with polyester fibres and then petrochemicals. Petroleum refining soon acquired oil and gas production band exploration plants. Reliance started growing as the largest conglomerate in India. In 1983, his younger son, Anil Ambani also joined the business as the CEO at Naroda.

And very soon, it held a name for itself even in the domestic market for its good quality products and with extensive endorsing of the same values in the Indian interiors. And there was no turning back since the dominance in the market began. He also delved into synthetic textiles when the commodities of his company were at their peak.

In 1975, a technical team from the **World Bank** also paid a visit to their textile mill.

Today, **Hazira Complex** is an active petrochemical complex located in Gujarat, India. According to GlobalData, who tracks more than 13,000 active and developing petrochemical plants worldwide, the complex started commercial operations in 1991 and currently has an active annual capacity of 7.15mtpa. Its capacity is expected to increase to 7.64mtpa in 2030. The plants are operated by Reliance Industries.

Building an Empire

Dhirubhai Ambani proposed for investing and finance from the National Banks, and on refusal, he made the company public in the year 1977. Dhirubhai also became the **first face of Indian business** who conquered the Industrial sector globally.

Reliance Launched its First IPO in India

In 1977, Reliance Industries Ltd. started the equity cult and launched its **first IPO in India** with an issue size of Rs.2.82 crores.

Dhirubhai Ambani successfully convinced middle-class investors that anyone investing in the company's IPO would get a massive return in the future. You won't believe what happened next! A whopping 58,000 middle-class investors invested in the Reliance IPO, and it got oversubscribed by seven times.

Reliance Goes Public

1977 saw Dhirubhai Ambani take **Reliance** public once nationalised banks shied away from financing him. His dexterity in navigating a stubborn economy that was upheld by stringent government regulations and bureaucracy was not appreciated at that time. As a result, he was accused of being corrupt and manipulating politics to work in his favour. Investor confidence, however, remained unaffected and this was at least partially owed to the fact that the company provided its investors with handsome dividends. Dhirubhai's vision and public perception only added to the company's appeal from the investors' perspective. By organising annual general meetings that were attended by thousands, his charisma had dazzled Indian investors. This saw itself play out with several of these meetings being organised in stadiums to accommodate the vast swathes of investors that descended upon him to hear what he had to say.

He also rallied with the **Bombay Stock Exchange** when he attained a huge profit from supplying his own shares to **The Bear Cartel**, who were trying to overtake him. There was a roar in the market about how he could make such a profit when the crisis fell on the entire nation. And to figure out the workings the Bombay office was closed for 3 days. And Pranab Mukherjee, the then Prime Minister also came to his defence about the stock market and Dhirubhai's works which were legal and by any means did not engage in unethical transaction procedures.

Even with many allegations of fraud and debauchery from the media and the market, the investors stood unshaken and trusted him. The investors never doubted Dhirubhai's capability as a businessman and their shares and dividends value only grew. He was truly a genius in the stock market and many people attended his meetings where he talked about it to gain knowledge. In fact, because of massive crowds and many attendees from all the sectors, the meetings were held in stadiums and even televised to be aired for people who couldn't make it in person.

Chapter - 6

Final Years

In the 1980s, Dhirubhai handed over Reliance to his sons, Mukesh and Anil Ambani. Mukesh Ambani expanded the company even further than Dhirubhai was able to do so. Today, the conglomerate is called **Reliance Industries Limited** and has offerings that include shopping, dining and hospitality, electric vehicle charging and battery swapping stations, fleet management solutions, integrated payment platform, jet/aviation turbine fuel, transportation fuels, auto LPG and lubricants.

While Dhirubhai Ambani did not get to see the entire extent to which Reliance expanded under the leadership of his sons, it was still extremely successful at the time of his death in 2002.

Dhirubhai Ambani truly embodies greatness and humility in equal measure. Even after achieving so much wealth and fortune he always celebrated his roots and took pride in them. It is not easy to start from scratch and build an empire that lasts several generations. With support from his family, he was unstoppable. India takes pride in an entrepreneur like him that comes rarely.

Chapter - 7

Demise

Dhirubhai Ambani was admitted to the Breach Candy Hospital in Mumbai on 24th June 2002 after he suffered a second stroke. The first stroke had occurred in February 1986 which led to paralysis of his right hand. He was in coma for more than a week and several doctors were consulted. He breathed his last on July 6th 2002.

Never before had an industrialist's death brought such a crowd at the funeral. But then Dhirubhai Ambani was no mere industrialist.

Indeed, the collective stream of visitors had begun with the news of his hospitalisation on June 24th . Mumbai's Breach Candy Hospital had become a gathering ground of politicians, industrialists, film stars - it seemed as if there was no one whose life Dhirubhai had not touched.

The trust and faith in the man was almost infinite. A businessman who had known him closely summed it up best, **"If the doctors can just get him back to his senses, Dhirubhai will pull through. We have faith in his will-power."**

But it was not to be. The man who wouldn't ever give up, finally went down fighting the grim battle for survival for 13 days at the Breach Candy Hospital in Mumbai. The end came finally at 11:50 p.m. on Saturday. At 7.30 a.m. Dhirubhai's body was brought to his residence, Sea Wind, at Cuffe Parade in south-Mumbai where it was kept for last respects while children Mukesh, Anil, Nina and Dipti and daughters-in-law Nita and Tina stood by.

And thousands turned up to pay their last respects . From the leaders of India Inc to the stars of Bollywood, from the politicians and senior bureaucrats to shareholders and employees, from children in parents' arms to the old carried in chairs, from Ratan Tata to Amitabh Bachchan to Bal Thackeray, from emissaries, from the Prime Minister to the leader of opposition and ministers and Chief Ministers cutting across party lines through the special gate that was set up for VIPs to enter away from the crowds that were thronging the main gate.

By around 3.30 p.m. people were asked to leave the premises so that arrangements could be made to take the body for cremation, but outside the crowds just swelled, pleading with the security guards to allow them in.

The body was taken to Marine Lines in an open truck with sons and family members and associates standing beside brothers Mukesh and Anil. but the streets were packed with thousands of people - on trees, on the footover bridge, even on electric poles. For the last 15 metres, Dhirubhai's body was carried on his sons' shoulders. At 6 p.m. it was taken inside the crematorium.

"Dhirubhaiji amar rahe (Long live Dhirubhai)" screamed the crowds as many lunged towards the body, just to touch it, in the hope perhaps that his Midas touch would rub off on them, struggling towards his body, braving police lathis.

Many of these may have been those who had become lakhpatis by merely buying his company's shares at the right time. But there were many to whom he was an idol to be emulated. A real story in a city that sells tinsel dreams of rags to riches.

"Dhirubhai will go one day," he had said in an interview long back, **"but Reliance's employees and shareholders will keep it afloat. Reliance is now a concept in which the Ambanis have become irrelevant."**

Mukesh and Anil Ambani, his sons who have largely been responsible for Reliance's meteoric rise since Dhirubhai's first stroke in the 80s, have not become irrelevant, but Dhirubhai does leave behind a concept that has captured the imagination of many an entrepreneur: can do.

Chapter - 8

Post-Death of Dhirubhai Ambani

After Dhirubhai Ambani passed away in 2002, disputes started arising between the two brothers, Mukesh and Anil Ambani. So, they split in December 2005, and Anil Ambani formed the **"Reliance Group"** while Mukesh Ambani continued expanding **"Reliance Industries."**

At present, Reliance Industries is highly successful and has its wings in the following sectors:-

1. Textiles

2. Petrochemicals

3. Telecom

4. Energy

5. Electricity

6. Retail

7. Digital Services

8. Logistics

9. Industrial Infrastructure

Chapter - 9

Honours and Recognitions

Dhirubhai Ambani was a highly accomplished businessman and during the course of his life, he was conferred with many honours and recognitions.

In 2016, Dhirubhai Ambani was honoured with the second highest civilian award, **Padma Vibhushan**, for his excellent contribution to the Indian market and its economy.

In an unauthorized biography, by an Australian journalist, Hamish McDonald in 1988, Dhirubhai was referred to and rightly so as, **'The Polyester Prince.'**

He was also awarded a **Lifetime Achievement Award** in 2001 by **The Economic Times Awards** on August 10th in Mumbai.

He became the first Indian ever, to receive the **"Dean's Medal"** by **The Wharton School, University of Pennsylvania**, in 1998 on June 15th for setting a remarkable example in leadership.

He was also featured in the **Asiaweek magazine** for 3 years, **1996, 1998** and **2000** in the list of 50 most "powerful people of Asia."

He was conferred with the honour of **"Man of the Century"** in November 2000 in Mumbai. The award was conferred by **Chemtech Foundation** and **Chemical Engineering World** for making an outstanding contribution to the Chemical industry in India.

The **Federation of Indian Chambers of Commerce and Industry** named Dhirubhai Ambani as **'Man of the 20th Century.'**

A **postal stamp** was released by **India Post** on 28th December 2002 featuring Dhirubhai Ambani.

In Oct 2011, Dhirubhai Ambani was posthumously awarded the **ABLF Global Asian Award** at the Asian Business Leadership Forum Awards.

Chapter - 10

How Dhirubhai Ambani had a historic defeat against Larsen & Toubro?

In 1987, a sense of apprehension broke out in L&T, when a Dubai-based businessman named Manu Chhabria bought a 1% stake in the company. Afraid of Manu's hostile takeovers, NM Desai, the former chairman of L&T, approached business tycoon Dhirubhai Ambani for help. Dhirubhai saved L&T by acquiring an 18.5% stake for approx Rs. 190 crore over the next 2 years. Both young Mukesh and Anil were given Board seats at L&T.

However, Dhirubhai's true intentions showed up when he got elected as the Chairman, and NM Desai got kicked out from his own company. L&T was a cash-rich entity and so he used a line of credit to buy huge chunks of RIL shares for L&T.

When VP Singh became the Prime Minister in 1989, he brought back government control in L&T via LIC, obstructing every move the Ambanis made. Dhirubhai had no option but to eventually leave his Chairmanship. Despite Congress's return in 1991, Dhirubhai couldn't make a comeback because of the indirect hindrance caused by the then Finance Minister, Dr. Manmohan Singh via LIC.

In 2001, Reliance exited from L&T by selling its stake to KM Birla's Grasim industries, and for the first time, Dhirubhai lost a business battle.

Chapter - 11

Achievements and Awards

Dhirubhai earned numerous prestigious awards including 'Man of the Century award', 'Dean's Medal,' and 'Lifetime Achievement Award.'

1. Conferred the **Lifetime Achievement Award** by India HRD Congress in February 2002.

2. Conferred **The Economic Times** award for corporate excellence for lifetime achievement in August 2001.

3. Thrice rated as '**India's Most Admired CEO**' in the Business Barons-Taylor Nelson Sofres-Mode survey in June 2001, 2000 and 1999.

4. Felicitated by the **Brihamumbai Municipal Corporation**, the biggest civic body of the country, with a citation and address followed by civic reception in December 2002.

5. Conferred the '**Man of the Century**' award by Chemtech Foundation and Chemical Engineering world in recognition of his outstanding contribution to the growth and development of the chemical industry in India, in November 2000.

6. Conferred the '**Indian Entrepreneur of the 20th Century**' award by FICCI for his meticulous scripting of one of the most remarkable stories of business endeavours, in March 2000.

7. Thrice nominated as one of the '**Power 50 - The Most Powerful People in Asia**' by Asiaweek magazine in 2000, 1998 and 1996.

8. Voted as the '**Most Admired Indian of the Millennium**' in the field of business and economics' in 'Legends - a celebration of Excellence' poll audited by Ernst and Young for Zee network in January 2000.

9. Voted as '**Creator of Wealth of the Century**' in 'The Times of India' poll in January 2000.

10. Chosen as one of three '**makers of equity**' by 'India Today' in their special millennium issue entitled '100 people who shaped India in the 20th Century' in January 2000.

11. Chosen by the Indian Merchants Chamber as '**an outstanding visionary of the 20th century**' for his achievements and contribution to the development of industry and capital markets in India, in December 1999.

12. Voted as '**Indian Businessman of the Century**' in Business Barons Global Multimedia poll December 1999.

13. Amongst the '**Power 50- India's 50 most powerful decision maker in politics, business and finance**' in Business Barons in August 1999.

14. Declared '**Most admired Indian business leader**' by The Times of India, indiatimes.com poll in July 1999.

15. The only Indian industrialist in the '**Business Hall of Fame**' in Asia Week in October 1998.

16. Awarded the **Dean's Medal by the Wharton School, University of Pennslyvania**, for setting an outstanding example of leadership, in June 1998.

17. Chosen as '**Star of Asia**' by Business Week, USA in June 1998.

18. **Business Barons** placed Ambani on its list of India's 25 Most influential business and financial leaders, in June 1998.

19. Awarded the **Companion Membership of Textile Institute, UK**, a membership which is limited to 50 living members, who have substantially advanced the general interests of industries based in fibres, in 1994.

20. Chosen '**Businessman of the year 1993**' by Business India, in January 1994.

Chapter - 12

Major Works

Dhirubhai Ambani was the originator, and every visualization was his cultivation behind laying the foundation of **Reliance Group**. From working small to reaching this position, he made his name written in history, he made this business the largest growing business in India.

Dhirubhai brought a revolutionary change in the capital market functioning, many retail investors were brought by him in the market who had domination of some big financial institutions. He introduced a new culture, the culture of equity to India. Those who were agreed to trust in his companies would return their trust in form of a bomb of wealth. It became the first-ever Indian organization/company to be featured on Forbes 500 list.

Chapter - 13

What We Can Learn From His Life?

Grab opportunity:-

Opportunities never wait for someone, if you want people to appreciate you on your success then grab the opportunity before someone else grabs it. From childhood to young age he always did surprising works by taking the proper steps and grabbing the opportunities, this quality made him an inspiration for all of us.

Be kind but never spread a word about it:-

It's said that Dhirubhai never spread a word about how and who he helped, he never believed in gaining publicity through charity instead he used to help people silently, even the people who were being helped by him was sometimes unknown about the helper, such generous behaviour should be adopted by everyone, be he a true leader or an ordinary human.

The upgrading is necessary:-

He believed in upgrading - be it in business or life, he wasn't contented by one business and always strived for more, through which he could make a small firm into the largest conglomerate in India. He believed it is up to us to upgrade and build our empire or just live in the same place for a lifetime.

Determination is the key:-

It was a time when there was no buyer for his fabric and buyers refused to buy, then he came out on the roads to sell the product to the retailers directly. This was his determination towards his dream which made his company grow faster and earn higher profits. Similarly, we should cultivate such determination and passion to attain success.

Chapter - 14

Business Secrets of Dhirubhai Ambani, Founder of Reliance Industries

Dhirubhai Ambani, the founder of Reliance Industries, was a genius who had extraordinary talent. He was creative and mastered the secrets of business, a pioneer among businessmen in India. He wrote his own story and became a hero of his century, changing the shape of Indian business and investing.

This Indian business icon had a real rag to riches story and was undoubtedly the most talented businessman of his time. He amazed the world. Born in Gujarat, he became a celebrity in India and overseas. Kokilaben Ambani, his devoted wife, supported him and always remained behind him in all his achievements.

What were the secrets of his amazing growth? What made him Dhirubhai Ambani? How did he become an industrial tycoon and a global conglomerate? Why does he have fans in India, the US, China, Japan, the UK, the EU, Canada, and elsewhere?

His Business Secrets

There are seven business secrets of his success in the corporate world.

1. Gather Information Whatever It May Be

- Gather information about governments, local, state, central and international

- Do not forget to get information about your competitors

- Gather information about products, companies, consumers, markets, people, services, and politics

He was able to quickly gather, process, and analyze information and disburse it to his subordinates when and where required. Through the information, he was able to find new opportunities.

Prof. ML Sisodia, one of my friends and a senior professor of physics and a research scholar, once told me a story about Dhirubhai Ambani. Mr. Sisodia had undergone a bypass surgery after a heart attack. A few days after his surgery, his son was called for an interview with Dhirubhai Ambani.

Dhirubhai wanted him for a senior position in his company. The very first question Dhirubhai Ambani asked him was, "How is your father?" This instance alone is enough to show his capability to gather information, even though it was not yet the internet age.

2. Find Opportunity

He always endeavored to analyze whatever information he had. He would convert information into profit-making opportunities. According to him, "There is no invitation for making profits." You have to find it.

3. Jump From One Orbit to the Next

No matter where you are, just work there. Master that place or situation. Accumulate some energy and then jump into a higher orbit. Stay there for some time and control it and master it. Then, jump to another, higher level, the next orbit.

Dhirubhai did this many times during his life. Caution: Do not jump from one orbit to another without mastering the present orbit. This could be dangerous. Be patient.

4. Complete Projects On Time

Learn to finish before the scheduled time. He and his sons completed all their projects on time or even beforehand. It didn't matter how big the projects were or how many hurdles they faced, they still completed them in a timely manner.

Dhirubhai Ambani and his sons Mukesh and Anil developed some techniques to make sure they were always on time, monitoring their projects closely.

5. Think Big- Think Global

He was thinking global even before the current trend of globalization. Most Indian companies were not doing well in the global scenario at his time and were not acting with global standards.

He made world-class projects and world-class companies. Nobody in India was even thinking about that at the time.

6. Hire the Best People. Pay Them Well

Dhirubhai Ambani was able to employ the best, top-ranking people in every field. He was an excellent employer, never compromising on quality or timeliness. He could only do what he did with the best people. According to him, human resources are the most important resources.

7. Pay Shareholders Well

His ambitious projects needed a lot of capital but bankers and financiers failed to trust his capabilities. They were reluctant and did not agree to fund his projects because they were risky.

So Dhirubhai Ambani went to his shareholders since he recognized them as the best source of funding and asked them for money. The shareholders jumped at the chance to fund his projects and he paid them handsomely, rewarding them for their trust.

He realized that shareholders would never be satisfied with dividends that matched the trend at the time. He knew the value of capital appreciation so he paid bonuses, and issued rights to his shareholders in addition to regular dividends.

Dhirubhai Went Beyond Investors' Expectations

He went beyond the expectations of his investors. He even went to the extent of challenging the law. Once he converted non-convertible debentures into shares, creating an enormous profit even though it was against the law. He fought against that law and the government was compelled to change it.

In his time, he had the highest number of shareholders. He boosted the market capitalization of BSE and brought millions of shareholders under his umbrella, many of them first-time investors.

Teachings Of Dhirubhai Ambani

Dhirubhai Ambani followed these secret techniques of business throughout his lifetime. He was not very interested in books or magazines about management. Rather, he left those for his subordinates and his managers. He had an appetite, a never-ending hunger for news.

Starting as a low-level employee of a gas station, he became an industrial giant, a global conglomerate. His name was included in the Fortune 500 and he could manage a yearly revenue of $78 billion. At that time, no other Indian industrialist had achieved something like that. But he was not satisfied—he was dreaming of being the world's richest person. He only did not achieve this because of his untimely death.

However, it has been achieved through Reliance Industries, which he founded. Soon after his death, the combined assets of Mukesh and Anil Ambani (the sons of Dhirubhai Ambani, between whom his assets were distributed) reached to a stage, more than Bill Gates of the Microsoft Corporation.

Chapter - 15

Life Of Dhirubhai Ambani With His Wife, Kokilaben Ambani

Dhirubhai Ambani and Kokilaben Ambani were that one power couple, who had never let their success and money affect their grounded nature and humbleness. The simple lady from Jamnagar had not only played a significant role in her husband's journey to success but as the matriarch of the family, she had stood by her values and made a settlement between her sons, Mukesh Ambani and Anil Ambani post the demise of Dhirubhai Ambani.

In one of her rare interviews, Kokilaben Ambani had spoken about her life in Jamnagar, married life with Dhirubhai Ambani, her belief in the importance of evolving and her domestic life. In an interview with the Mid-Day, Kokilaben Ambani had begun with reminiscing her childhood memories in Jamnagar and had recalled:

"I spent my childhood in Jamnagar, which was not as developed those years as it is now. We were a middle-class family. I would do all the household chores that girls of those days were expected to do. I would also do sewing and embroidery work. Our elders believed that girls should be well versed in domestic chores."

Married Life with Dhirubhai Ambani

Speaking of her married life with Dhirubhai Ambani and her life with him in Aden, when they had shifted there for some time, Kokilaben Ambani had said:

"When I got married to Dhirubhai Ambani in 1955, I had not even dreamt that my life would change so much. I saw Mumbai for the first time. While going to Aden, (a city in Yemen) I marvelled at

the steamer, which was to take me there, once again, it was a first for me. Life in Aden (where Dhirubhai lived for some time) was so different compared to Jamnagar or other places but Dhirubhai was my guide. Aden was a turning point in the real sense for me. I became a mother for the first time. Mukesh was born in Aden (Anil, Dipty and Nina were born in Mumbai). All four of them were married in Mumbai. Today, ours is a family of 19 including two daughters-in-law, two sons-in-law and our nine grandchildren."

Long-Distance Relationship

Revealing what she liked the most in her husband, Dhirubhai Ambani and sharing an anecdote of a letter he had written to her from Aden when she was living in Chorwad, Kokilaben Ambani remarked:

"When I rewind to my earlier years, a number of anecdotes come back like the time when I was in Chorwad (in Gujarat) living there after my marriage. Dhirubhai had written a letter to me from Aden, which said, Kokila, I have bought a car and I will come to fetch you in that car. Can you guess what is the colour of the car? He then added, 'it is black, like me.' I liked his sense of humour the most. He came to pick me up in that car when I reached Aden. So it was a bullock cart at Chorwad, car at Aden and plane and helicopter in Mumbai."

Soon, their lives changed when Dhirubhai Ambani had moved to Mumbai and how he had made sure that his wife, Kokilaben Ambani was by his side every time, was indeed inspiring. Praising how he used to keep her with him on every step, shoulder to shoulder, Mrs Ambani had said:

"Immediately after coming to Mumbai my life changed rapidly. We were in the post-Independence phase, Dhirubhai was making headway. Once Reliance was set up, newer directions opened up for us. Dhirubhai was going up step-by-step and what is interesting is that he would keep me with him on every step, shoulder to shoulder. He would always keep me apprised and updated on his new projects and I would attend the inauguration of every plant. He would insist on me accompanying him to every party and function. He would often say meeting others would add to our general knowledge. Even when some dignitaries dropped by at our house, he would insist on me joining him."

Encouraging Husband

Crediting her husband, Dhirubhai Ambani for being the reason behind her adapting the changes in life with ease, encouraging her to learn English, introducing her to different cuisines and filling her up with the information of the places they used to visit, Kokilaben Ambani had remarked:

"Even though I had studied in a Gujarati school, I had started learning English immediately after coming to Mumbai. This was also thanks to Dhirubhai's foresight. A tutor used to come in to teach English to the children. Dhirubhai said, Kokila why don't you learn English? I jumped at the suggestion. He would take me to five-star hotels so that I could cultivate a taste for Chinese, Mexican, Italian and Japanese cuisine. Even when we went abroad, he would fill me in with information about the places we visited and even asked me to read about them. In short, he moulded me so well, that I would not feel out of place anywhere. I constantly adapted to change."

How she wishes things to be different in terms of technology and science back then as compared to now, Kokilaben Ambani had shared:

"Often, I would wish I were born late in the world, so that I could have reaped the benefits of new inventions in science and technology. I sometimes rue that when I was in Chorwad and Dhirubhai in Aden, letters exchanged between us would reach so late. It would have been so much better in the age of rapid communication. Again, when I was going to Aden by steamer, I was alone, longing for my parents and siblings. I often think if I had a mobile then...I do use the computer, i Phone with ease now, but I want to learn to make a greater, more efficient use of the computer."

Speaking about the 'modern woman' and how she had learnt immensely from her husband, Dhirubhai Ambani, Kokilaben Ambani had said:

"When I am asked about modern women and their time management, their dexterity in handling several responsibilities at once like family, home, children, I would say that the modern woman herself is worth emulating. Speaking for myself, I would say that I am a student of the Dhirubhai Ambani University - I have learnt immensely from my late husband. I would like to finish by saying that my belief in God is so strong, I do not think even a leaf can move without His sanction. My mother would often say, if it

works out in our favour it is God's blessing and if it does not, it is his wish."

Kokilaben Ambani has given an insight in the life of her late husband, Dhirubhai Ambani in the book she had written, which is titled, **Dhirubhai Ambani: The Man I Knew** in the English version and **Dhirubhai Ambani: Maara Jeevan Sathi** in the Gujarati edition. Mrs Ambani had described the story of Dhirubhai Ambani's life and his meteoric rise in business as well as personal life. She had also elaborated on her life with the man, who, in her belief, was born to be a legend in his own time. She had written:

"During all those years, I had never seen him in a miserable or a desperate state of mind. That does not mean he never faced difficulties. But when engulfed by difficulty, he used to resolve it with courage and imagination."

The Family Man

Not only his determination and struggle to reach the very pinnacle of success, but Kokilaben Ambani had also thrown light on how Dhirubhai Ambani had devoted time and energy to his children's learning and to the development of their personalities. She had written:

"Everyday, over dinner, he would take time out to update himself on what his children were doing (and learning) and to encourage them to further expand their horizons. He took the word 'impossible' out of his grandchildren's vocabulary and inspired them to see the world as a place of exciting and limitless opportunity -- "a place where you could make things happen not because you were wealthy but because you were had the courage, boldness and initiative."

Just how Dhirubhai Ambani had fulfilled every responsibility and role with perfection in his professional life, in personal life too, he was a doting husband, a caring father and a loving grandfather. The way he had supported and encouraged his wife throughout their married life and how he had made sure she was by he side at every step is what terms like 'better-half', sheer 'couple goals' and 'life partner' mean in the truest sense!

Chapter - 16

Dhirubhai Ambani's Children

Mukesh Dhirubhai Ambani, born on 19th April 1957 is the eldest son of Dhirubhai Ambani and is currently the Chairman and Managing Director of Reliance Industries, a Fortune Global 500 company. According to **Bloomberg Billionaires Index**, Ambani's net worth is estimated at $83.4 billion as of February 2023, making him the richest person in Asia and the 13th richest person in the world.

Education

Mukesh Ambani attended the Hill Grange High School at Peddar Road, Mumbai, along with his brother Anil Ambani and Anand Jain, who later became his close associate. After his secondary schooling, he studied at St. Xavier's College, Mumbai. He then received a BE degree in chemical engineering from the Institute of Chemical Technology.

He later enrolled for an MBA at Stanford University but withdrew in 1980 to help his father build Reliance, which at the time was still a small but fast-growing enterprise. His father felt that real-life skills were harnessed through experiences and not by sitting in a classroom, so he called his son back to India from Stanford to take command of a yarn manufacturing project in his company.

Business Career

In 1981, he started to help his father Dhirubhai Ambani run their family business, **Reliance Industries Limited**. By this time, it had already expanded so that it also dealt in refining and petrochemicals. The business also included products and services in the retail and telecommunications industries. **Reliance Retail Ltd.**, another subsidiary, is also the largest retailer in India. **Reliance's Jio** has earned a top-five spot in the country's telecommunication services since its public launch on 5th September 2016.

As of 2016, Mukesh Ambani was ranked as the 36th richest person in the world, and has consistently held the title of India's richest person on **Forbes magazine's list** for the past ten years. He is the only Indian businessman on Forbes' list of the world's most powerful people. As of October 2020, Mukesh Ambani was ranked by Forbes as the 6th-wealthiest person in the world. He surpassed Jack Ma, executive chairman of Alibaba Group, to become Asia's richest person with a net worth of $44.3 billion in July 2018. He is also the wealthiest person in the world outside North America and Europe. As of 2015, he ranked fifth among India's philanthropists, according to China's Hurun Research Institute. He was appointed as a **Director of Bank of America** and became the first non-American to be on its board.

Through Reliance, he also owns the **Indian Premier League** franchise **Mumbai Indians** and is the founder of the **Indian Super League**, a football league in India. In 2012, Forbes named him one of the richest sports owners in the world. He resides at the Antilia, one of the world's most expensive private residences with its value reaching $1 billion.

Timeline - 1980s–1990s

In 1980, the Indian government under Indira Gandhi opened PFY (polyester filament yarn) manufacturing to the private sector. Dhirubhai Ambani applied for a license to set up a PFY manufacturing plant. Obtaining the license was a long-drawn-out process requiring a strong connection within the bureaucracy system because the government, at the time, was restricting large-scale manufacturing, making the importation of yarn for the textiles impossible. In spite of stiff competition from Tatas, Birlas and 43 others, Dhirubhai was awarded the license, more commonly addressed as License Raj. To help him build the PFY plant, Dhirubhai pulled his eldest son out of Stanford in 1981, where he was studying for his MBA, to work with him in the company. Ambani did not return to his university program, as he was in charge of Reliance's vertical integration, from textiles into polyester fibers and further into petrochemicals, which the yarns were made from. After joining the company, he reported daily to Rasikbhai Meswani, then executive director. The company was being built from scratch with the principle of everybody contributing to the business and not heavily depend on selected individuals. Dhirubhai treated him as a business partner allowing him the freedom to contribute even with little experience. This principle came into play after Rasikbhai's death in 1985 along with Dhirubhai suffering a stroke in 1986 when all the responsibility shifted to Mukesh Ambani and his brother. Mukesh Ambani set up Reliance Infocomm Limited (now Reliance Communications Limited), which was focused on information and communications technology initiatives. At the age of 24, Mukesh Ambani was given charge of the construction of Patalganga petrochemical plant when the company was heavily investing in oil refinery and petrochemicals.

2000–present

On 6th July 2002, Mukesh's father died after suffering a second stroke, which elevated tensions between the brothers as Dhirubhai had not left a will for the distribution of the empire in 2004.Their mother intervened to stop the feud, splitting the company into two, Mukesh receiving control of Reliance Industries Limited and Indian Petrochemicals Corporation Limited, which was later approved by the Bombay High Court in December 2005.

Mukesh Ambani directed and led the creation of the world's largest grassroots petroleum refinery at Jamnagar, India, which had the capacity to produce 660,000 barrels per day (33 million tonnes per year) in 2010, integrated with petrochemicals, power generation, port, and related infrastructure. In December 2013, he announced, at the Progressive Punjab Summit in Mohali, the possibility of a "collaborative venture" with Bharti Airtel in setting up digital infrastructure for the 4G network in India. On 18th June 2014, Mukesh Ambani, while addressing the 40th AGM of Reliance Industries, said he will invest Rs 1.8 trillion (short scale) across businesses in the next three years and launch 4G broadband services in 2015.

He was elected as a member into the National Academy of Engineering in 2016 for engineering and business leadership in oil refineries, petrochemical products, and related industries. In February 2016, Ambani-led Jio launched its own 4G smartphone brand named LYF. In June 2016, it was India's third-largest-selling mobile phone brand. The release of the service Reliance Jio Infocomm Limited, commonly known as Jio, in September 2016 was a success, and Reliance's shares increased. During the 40th annual general meeting of RIL, he announced bonus shares in the ratio of 1:1 which is the country's largest bonus issue in India, and announced the Jio Phone at an effective price of ₹0. As of February 2018, Bloomberg's "Robin Hood Index" estimated that Ambani's personal wealth was enough to fund the operations of the Indian federal government for 20 days.

In February 2014, a First Information Report (FIR) alleging criminal offenses was filed against Mukesh Ambani for alleged irregularities in the pricing of natural gas from the KG basin. Arvind Kejriwal, who had a short stint as Delhi's chief minister and had ordered the FIR, has accused various political parties of being silent on the gas price issue. Kejriwal has asked both Rahul Gandhi and Narendra Modi to clear their stand on the gas pricing issue. Kejriwal has alleged that the Centre allowed the price of gas to be inflated to eight dollars a unit though Mukesh Ambani's company spends only one dollar to produce a unit, which meant a loss of Rs. 540 billion to the country annually.

In August 2022, Ambani announced a $25bn plan for launching 5G mobile internet services in the next two months. High-speed internet will be launched in major cities such as New Delhi and Mumbai and then in the rest of the country by the end of 2023.

Stock Manipulation and Penalty

For manipulating shares of Reliance Petroleum Limited (RPL), **Reliance Industries** was fined Rs. 950 crore (about 447 crore in retracted gains and 500 crore in interest) in 2007. In April 2006, RPL went public as a Reliance subsidiary at a price of Rs. 60 per share. The market crashed by 30% after it floated at roughly Rs. 100, and RPL was back at 60. In accordance with **Securities and Exchange Board of India** directive, RIL carried out an organised operation with the help of its agents in order to obtain unauthorised profits from the trading of its formerly listed unit, RPL, which was combined with the former in 2009.

Anil Dhirubhai Ambani, born on 4th June 1959 is the Chairman, Managing Director and CEO of **Reliance Group.** The Reliance Group was created in July 2006 following a demerger from Reliance Industries Limited. He leads a number of stocks listed corporations including Reliance Capital, Reliance Infrastructure, Reliance Power and Reliance Communications.

Education

Anil Ambani earned his Bachelor of Science degree from Kishinchand Chellaram College and received a Master in Business Administration at the Wharton School of the University of Pennsylvania in 1983.

Business Career

Anil Ambani received parts of Reliance Group with interests in telecom, entertainment, financial services, power and infrastructure. He is also credited with India's largest IPO, that of Reliance Power, which in 2008 was subscribed in less than 60 seconds, the fastest in the history of Indian capital markets to date.

In 2005, Anil Ambani made his debut in the entertainment industry with an acquisition of a majority stake in **Adlabs Films,** a company with interests in film processing, production, exhibition and digital cinema. The company was renamed **Reliance MediaWorks** in 2009. In 2008, a joint venture worth US$1.2 billion with Steven Spielberg's production company **DreamWorks** cast his entertainment business on to a global platform. He has contributed to the production of several Spielberg films, including the Academy Award-winning Lincoln.

He gained notoriety as one of the fastest destroyers of shareholder wealth in the last 100 years with the combined group market cap declining by 90% since the formation of the **Reliance ADA Group.**

In early 2019, a court in Mumbai held him in criminal contempt for non-payment of personally guaranteed debt Reliance Communications owed to Swedish gear maker, Ericsson. Instead of jail, the court gave him a month to come up with the funds. At the end of the month, Ambani was bailed out by his elder brother, Mukesh Ambani.

In April 2019, three ADAG Companies reached standstill agreement with Franklin Templeton after secured NCD default. This led to SEBI changing mutual fund regulation of reducing unlisted NCDs exposure to 10% and making standstill agreement void. In aftermath, FT India didn't sell the pledged securities and wound 6 debt funds affecting 300,000 investors.

In February 2020, Anil Ambani was locked in a legal battle with 3 Chinese banks. He was asked to set aside US$100 million by the court which led him to make the statement that his net worth is currently zero after considering his liabilities. The dispute still rages on with the UK court ordering him to pay the 3 Chinese banks to the tune of US$716 million.

In October 2021, Anil Ambani was named in the **Pandora Papers** along with his brother Mukesh. In January 2023, the Bombay High Court questioned the Income Tax Department's accusation of tax evasion against Anil Ambani after a petition by him challenged the decision of the notice issued by the IT department.

Allegations of Political Connections

In 2018, India's principal opposition party, Indian National Congress, accused Prime Minister, Narendra Modi of favouring Anil Ambani's defence manufacturing company over HAL, a public sector enterprise, in a fighter aircraft deal worth ₹58,000 crore (equivalent to ₹660 billion or US$8.3 billion in 2020) with French manufacturing firm Dassault. Ambani, several of whose companies are debt-ridden, has denied all charges of benefiting from crony capitalism. In factual terms, Reliance Defence stood to get just over 3 per cent of the ₹30,000 crore (equivalent to ₹340 billion or US$4.3 billion in 2020) Dassault Aviation offsets contract, contrary to the impression that it was to be the biggest beneficiary of the Rafale fighter jet deal.

In a possibly related controversy, one of his businesses partly financed a French film in which former French president Francois Hollande's then-partner had acted around the same time the aircraft deal was being negotiated.

Deepti Salgaocar is the youngest of the Ambani siblings. She was born on January 23rd 1962, to Dhirubhai Ambani and Kokilaben. Deepti Salgaocar studies law at VM Salgaocar College of Law. She is married to Duttaraj Salgaocar, a businessman. The two got married in 1983 and settled at the Salgaocar family mansion.

Nina Kothari is an Indian entrepreneur and daughter of Dhirubhai Ambani. Nina Kothari founded a coffee and food chain called **Javagreen** in 2003. Nina Kothari married businessman Bhadrashyam Kothari in 1986. Nina Kothari has two children, a son-- Arjun Kothari and a daughter-- Nayantara Kothari.

After the demise of her husband, Nina Kothari took the responsibility of their family business, **Kothari Sugars and Chemicals** into her own hand. She was appointed the Chairperson on April 8th 2015. According to corporate shareholdings, Nina Bhadrashyam Kothari holds two stocks publically and has a net worth of more than Rs 52.4 crores.

In Popular Media

In 1988, an unauthorized biography of Dhirubhai Ambani, by Hamish McDonald with the title, **The Polyester Prince**, outlined all his political and business conquests. The book was not published in India because the Ambanis threatened legal action; an updated version went on sale under the title Ambani and Sons in 2010, and there has been no action against the publisher so far.

A Hindi film said to be inspired by the life of Dhirubhai Ambani was released on 12th January 2007. **Guru**, directed by filmmaker Mani Ratnam, cinematography by Rajiv Menon and music by AR Rahman shows the struggle of a man striving to make his mark in the Indian business world with a fictional Shakti Group of Industries.

Chapter - 17

Dhirubhai Ambani's Candid Moment
With His Grand Kids

Grandparents are the most loving beings on this planet, and they leave no stone unturned to give their grand kids with all the happiness in this world. From spoiling them with their favourite toys to telling them bed-time stories and always delighting them with treats, the doting grandparents are always on their toes to bring a smile on their grand kids' faces. Needless to say, the moments spent with our grandparents are worth cherishing for a lifetime.

One of the greatest business tycoons, late Dhirubhai Ambani, was not just an excellent business magnate, but also a great human being. He and his wife, Kokilaben Ambani, are blessed with four kids, Mukesh Ambani, Anil Ambani, Dipti Salgaocar and Nina Kothari. Furthermore, they are doting grandparents to their grand kids, who respect them with all their heart. Late Dhirubhai Ambani used to dote on his grand kids.

Ambanis are well-known for treasuring their traditions and well-rooted heritage, and they never miss a chance to showcase it to the world. For instance, when Dhirubhai Ambani and Kokilaben Ambani's grandson, Anmol Ambani had got married, his loving wife, Khrisha Shah, sought the blessings of her ancestors as she became a part of the Ambani clan. On March 11th 2022, Tina Ambani had shared a priceless picture on her IG handle, in which she could be seen posing alongside her bahu, Khrisha Shah, her mother-in-law, Kokilaben Ambani, and the mega-portrait of late Dhirubhai Ambani. Along with the picture, Tina had penned a short note in the caption, and it could be read as:

"A new chapter begins for Anmol and Khrisha with blessings from friends and family - the wedding PC: @sam_and_ekta."

Chapter - 18

Reminiscences

Businessman Mukesh Ambani had once told in an interview, referring to the strict discipline of his father Dhirubhai Ambani, that he had locked him and his brother Anil Ambani in the garage.

Whenever it comes to the rich businessmen family in the country and abroad, then the Ambani family is included in this list. By the way, it is the strict rules of learning, ideology, and discipline of Dhirubhai Ambani, which have tied the Ambani family together till now. After the death of Dhirubhai Ambani, his property was divided between his two sons Mukesh Ambani and Anil Ambani. Today, Mukesh and Anil are carrying forward their father's legacy and are handling their respective businesses very well. However, once in their childhood both the brothers were locked in the garage by their father. Let us tell you the reason behind the whole story.

Once Mukesh Ambani had reached actress Simi Garewal's show **'Rendezvous with Simi Garewal'**. During this, he recalled his old struggling days, as well as the story when his father Dhirubhai Ambani locked him and his brother Anil in the garage. Mukesh had told that his father was very strict about discipline. Sharing the anecdote, Mukesh said that when he was 10 or 11 years old and Anil was 9 years old, one day in the evening some guests came to their house. When their mother Kokilaben brought food for the guests, it was destroyed by the two brothers. Seeing his mischief, his father asked him to sit quietly, but he did not listen to his father's words and later started jumping from one sofa to another in front of the guests. His father was very angry to see the children jumping like this.

Mukesh Ambani had further said that his father did not say anything to him in front of the guests, but the next morning his anger was on cloud nine. In such a situation, Dhirubhai Ambani had asked his two sons to go out of the house to teach them a lesson and said that from today both brothers will stay in the garage. Although Mukesh and Anil's mother Kokilaben took the side of her sons and recommended not to send them out of the house, Dhirubhai, who was very strict about his rules and regulations and discipline, did not listen to anyone and sent both his sons to the garage. During their stay in the garage, both the brothers were given only bread and water. Telling this story, Mukesh Ambani said that after this punishment of his father, he never did such mischief.

In the same interview, he also recalled his struggling days when he used to live in a room with nine people. However, due to the lessons and thinking given by his father, today Mukesh Ambani lives with his family in Mumbai's largest and most luxurious building **'Antilia'.**

Chapter - 19

Seven Lessons One Can Learn from Dhirubhai Ambani's Success Story

Here are seven lessons one can gather from "Dhirubhai Ambani's success story" that will help one grow in life:-

1. When there's a lot of confusion in your life, just follow your heart.

2. Taking risks is vital, but those risks should be "calculated risks."

3. Don't be afraid to leap. You can't even imagine how high you can fly.

4. Your planning should be patient, but your execution should be impatient.

5. Anyone, irrespective of any background, can have huge dreams.

6. You can learn anything if you truly want to.

7. While climbing the ladder to success, many people will try to pull you down out of envy. You just need to ignore them.

Chapter - 20

Business Rivalries

Business rivalries are common and when in the same industry, businessmen often collide. Almost everyone knows about the rivalry between Apple co-founder, Steve Jobs and Microsoft founder, Bill Gates. India has also seen its fair share of business rivalries over the years.

There is one man in India who battled with business giants like Dhirubhai Ambani and Ratan Tata and lived to tell the tale. Bombay Dyeing Chairman, Nusli Wadia was once engaged in corporate battles with Reliance founder, Dhirubhai Ambani and Tata Sons Chairman Emeritus, Ratan Tata.

Wadia vs Ambani: The most celebrated battle in Indian corporate history

Wadia's Bombay Dyeing was one of the textile kings during the pre-Ambani era. The corporate battle between Wadia and Ambani began when both looked at the polyester industry for growth. What started as a conflict later turned into a warfare. The Wadia vs Ambani corporate was termed by media as **'the ancient regime locking horns with the nouveau riche'.**

Wadia lost the war to Ambani partly because of making some bad choices with his polyester intermediates. For instance, he chose to produce dimethyl terephthalate (DMT) when Dhirubhai Ambani chose purified terephthalic acid (PTA). PTA turned out to be a more efficient intermediate in the manufacture of polyester.

In 2009, Wadia said he had no rivalry with the Ambani, debunking the perception the two business families were fierce adversaries. "I've no rivalry with him (Dhirubhai Ambani)... I'm just saying the rivalry is now at different levels... with different people... different issues," Wadia said in an interview when asked about the old rivalry between him and the late founder of the Reliance business empire.

Wadia vs Tata: From friends to foes

The Tata-Wadia corporate relationship has gone through several phases. Wadia has been friends with Ratan Tata since childhood. In fact, he used to consider JRD Tata, as his godfather and mentor. Not many people know that it was JRD Tata who had helped Wadia when Nusli wanted to acquire control of Bombay Dyeing.

Wadia, also known as a corporate **samurai**, guided Ratan Tata during the latter's initial years as Tata group chairman. The relationship between Wadia and Tata turned sour when Wadia decided to sue Ratan Tata. When the Mistry-Tata conflict was at its peak, Wadia backed Mistry and as a result, he was removed from the position of Tata Motors' independent director.

In 2016, Wadia filed a defamation case against Ratan Tata and Tata Group claiming that he was unfairly ousted from the Tata Motors as he never entered the dispute unless he felt wrong. An industrialist familiar with both the business groups was quoted in an HT report saying, "In fact, Wadia was an informal adviser to (Ratan) Tata when he (Tata) took on these mighty stalwarts and ousted them. It is ironical that Wadia and Tata are now fighting."

For those who are not aware, earlier this year, Wadia, who presides over a biscuits-to-aviation empire, withdrew the criminal defamation suit against Tata Sons and its board members and executives, including Ratan Tata. In doing so, he let go a potential Rs 3,000 crore that he had sought in reputational damages. In a 2009 interview with ET Now, when asked about fellow industrialist Ratan Tata, Wadia said, "Tata is a very dear friend... he is a friend, a family..."

It is worth mentioning that Wadia is known for his ability to fight as was displayed in his corporate battles in the with tycoons including Dhirubhai Ambani, Ratan Tata and Rajan Pillai of Brittania.

Chapter - 21

Reliance Family Day

Mukesh Ambani, the head of the country's most prestigious business group, **Reliance Industries Limited (RIL)**, has expressed confidence that the country can become a $ 40 trillion economy by the 100th anniversary of India's independence. In his virtual address to the Reliance family on the occasion of **Reliance Family Day,** Mukesh Ambani said that the coming 25 years are going to bring big changes for India with a 5000 year old civilization.

Company will continue to grow like 'Banyan'

Mukesh Ambani said on the occasion of **Family Day** that 45 years ago, the founder of Reliance Industries, Dhirubhai Ambani had planted the seed of this banyan tree. This company is growing like a 'Banyan tree'. He said, the branches of this banyan tree of Reliance Industries will spread even wider and the roots will be deeper.

Reliance will focus on these five sectors

Ambani also lauded the leadership of his son Akash Ambani and daughter Isha Ambani, who head Reliance Jio and Reliance Retail, respectively. He also mentioned on the occasion 5 key sectors on which the company will focus in the coming 25 years.

1. 5G Telecom

Mukesh Ambani said that under the leadership of Akash Ambani, Reliance's 5G is spreading across the country in a very short time. He said that by the end of 2023, **Jio** will have 5G network across the country. This speed is the highest compared to any other country in the world. With 5G we can now ensure that no Indian is denied access to high quality education, high quality healthcare and high productivity economic activities.

2. Retail Sector

The second sector that Ambani mentioned is the retail sector, which is being led by Isha Ambani. Mukesh Ambani claimed that under Isha's leadership, RIL's retail business "has grown exponentially." Reliance Retail has created over two lakh new jobs last year, making it one of India's leading employers. With the help of Reliance Retail, our youth will have more jobs. The income of our farmers will be more. Our SMEs and large manufacturers will become more productive. And our business-partners will be more prosperous.

3. O2C Business

O2C ie Isle to Business is the core business of Reliance. Mukesh Ambani said that we will continue to maintain our leadership position in the O2C business with new capabilities. He added that in the E&P segment, our team is working hard to provide energy security for India. He said, Reliance is excited about the media and entertainment business and its integration with digital services which will completely change the industry.

4. New Energy

Mukesh Ambani said that New Energy, Reliance's newest start-up business, has the potential to transform not only the company or the country, but the entire world. It shows that we care about the world, and we care about everyone in the world. With Anant Ambani joining this upcoming next-gen business, we are making rapid progress towards getting our **Giga Factories** ready in Jamnagar. From being India's largest and most valuable corporate, Reliance is now on its way to becoming India's 'Greenest' Corporate.

5. Reliance Foundation

2023 will also be a year of transformation for Reliance Foundation. Under the leadership of Nita Ambani, Reliance Foundation is working on even more ambitious new initiatives in education, healthcare, sports, women's empowerment and ecological conservation.

Chapter - 22

How Dhirubhai Ambani turned the tables on the Kolkata Bear Cartel?

India's biggest private sector company, **Reliance Industries Ltd** went public through its initial public offering (IPO) in October 1977, when it issued 2.8 million equity shares of Rs 10 each. Thereafter, the company frequently raised money through convertible debentures. As Hamish Mcdonald writes in his book, **Ambani and Sons**: "Thereafter Reliance expanded its equity base through frequent rights and bonus issues to shareholders...but it was through the use of convertible debentures that Dhirubhai (Ambani) made his big splash in the capital markets."

After the IPO, the share price of Reliance kept climbing. "In the first year of listing, 1978, Reliance had reached a high of Rs 50, five times the par value of the share, which was a high premium in those times. In 1980 it hit Rs 104...and in 1982 it reached a high of Rs 186." In early 1982 Reliance announced a rights issue of partly convertible debentures. Partially convertible debentures are used to borrow money from investors. They payout a certain rate of interest for a specific period and a part of those debentures is then converted into shares on a later date.

A cartel of bear operators , supposedly from Kolkata, started short selling shares of Reliance. Short selling is a transaction where investors sell shares they do not own, in the hope that the price of the share will fall and they can pick it up at a lower price and make delivery at a later date. As McDonald writes, "The selling pressure was intense on March 18, creating a half-hour of panic just before the close. The bears sold 350,000 Reliance shares, causing the price to fall quickly from Rs 131 to Rs 121."

SK Barua and JR Varma recall in their rather delightful book, **The Great Indian Scam – Story of the Missing Rs 4,000 crore**, "Just before the rights (issue) was to open for subscription , the bears sensed that the management of the company was artificially keeping the price of the shares high to ensure full subscription to the rights issue. Accordingly , they started short selling Reliance shares."

But then something strange happened. "A buying wave began. The more the bears sold – the numbers got to 1.1 million shares – the more NRI investors 'based in West Asian countries' picked up. Eventually they bought more than 800,000 shares sold by the bears," writes McDonald. This left everybody bewildered on who was buying Reliance shares. These investors evidently spent around Rs 10 crore buying Reliance shares.

During those days settlement of shares at the Bombay Stock Exchange used to happen every second Friday unlike the current T+3 working days settlement. So in this particular case the bears who had short sold Reliance shares, had to either deliver those shares on the settlement day or pay something known as an **undha badla**, in case they did not have the shares required for delivery, to carry over the transaction to the next settlement date.

On April 30th , the NRI investors who had been buying the shares of Reliance being short sold by the bears, demanded delivery of the shares. In case, the bears did not have the shares, the investors demanded an **undha badla** of Rs 25 per share. As McDonald writes "The bear cartel baulked, throwing the exchange into a crisis that shut it down until the following Wednesday. In the following days the price of Reliance shares rose to a peak of Rs 201 as the bear brokers located shares to fulfill their sales.

The need to make the delivery of Reliance shares ensured that the price of the Reliance shares remained high in the days to come. "The prices of Reliance shares remained high in the days following the incident because of persistent buying by the entrapped bears. It was rumored that the major supplier of share certificates to the market during that period was none other than the late Dhirubhai Ambani, the Chairman and Managing Director of the company. By merely routing his shares through the desperate bears, he extracted a handsome penalty through price difference. The bears bought the shares at high prices from him and delivered it back to him at the contracted price of Rs 150!" write Barua and Varma.

This story, other than giving us an example of Ambani's shrewdness, also tells us very clearly that in business it is necessary to deliver the knock-out punch to the enemy. And to deliver that knock-out punch it is very necessary for the CEO to have the ability to role up his sleeves, take things into their own hands and rescue the situation before it goes out of hand. And this is what made Dhirubhai, the successful man that he was.

Chapter - 23

Dhirubai Ambani's Legacy

At a gathering to celebrate 40 years of **Reliance Industries Ltd (RIL)**, the Chairman and Managing Director of the company, Shri Mukesh D Ambani, paid a rich tribute to Dhirubhai Ambani. He said that he learned four important lessons from him: **Courage, Empathy, Absolute Faith in Technology and Talent, and Dil Ka Rishta**. Due to these, he could steer RIL successfully to the newer heights, he said.

Today, on the 16th death anniversary of Dhirubhai, I remember how obsessed he was with state-of-the-art technologies in the plants he set up. His vision had no limits. He used to keep himself updated about newer discoveries, researches, and current trends in the sectors he operated in. This is why he could think much ahead of his time.

After coming back to India from Aden, he tried his hand in trading spices, yarn, etc, eventually making a foray into manufacturing. He set up **Greenfield textile unit** in Naroda, on the outskirts of Ahmedabad. He knew for certain, investment in technology could not fail. He firmly believed that technology assured high-quality products in a shorter period of time; consistency in quality was an added benefit.

Because of Dhirubhai's faith in technology, in 1975, Reliance Group's Naroda textile unit was recognised as '**The Most Modern Textile Complex of India**' by the World Bank. Ironically, it was a bad phase in the history of textile sector in Ahmedabad, as the mills had begun downing their shutters for some reason or the other. In such an adverse situation, the fabric manufactured using modern technology at Dhirubhai's unit became so acceptable and popular among masses that his textile brand **'Vimal'** became a household name overnight.

When Reliance set up its first refinery in Jamnagar, Dhirubhai had insisted on the use of the best and latest technology available at that time. The result? **RIL's Jamnagar Refinery** is considered one of the best refineries in the world with a very high complexity index. The Jamnagar refinery and petrochemical complex boasts of the highest Nelson Complexity Index of 14. Due to Dhirubai's insistence on the use of the latest and best technology, the Reliance refinery could cope with adverse market conditions that rose due to global geopolitical tensions.

The credit for making 4G VOLTE technology very popular in India also goes to **Reliance Jio**. The use of new technology created positive disruption in the telecom sector in the country, benefiting billions of telecom users. In addition, it played a pivotal role in realising Prime, Narendra Modi's **'Digital India'** dream.

*****